MW00767922

Hope For Today

Ten Week Devotional

Annette Herndon

PRESS

Copyright © 2008 by Annette Herndon

Hope For Today
Ten Week Devotional
by Annette Herndon

Printed in the United States of America

ISBN 978-1-60647-433-4

All rights reserved solely by the author. The author guarantees all contents are original and do not infringe upon the legal rights of any other person or work. No part of this book may be reproduced in any form without the permission of the author. The views expressed in this book are not necessarily those of the publisher.

Unless otherwise indicated, Bible quotations are taken from The New International Bible, Copyright © 1973, 1978, 1984 by International Bible Society and The Holy Bible, King James Version.

www.annetteherndon.com

www.xulonpress.com

Dedication

This book is lovingly dedicated to my father and mother, Jerry and Joyce McElhannon, to whom I am eternally grateful for raising me in a Godly home in which going to church and serving God was not an option. To my wonderful husband and greatest cheerleader, Harold Herndon whose tireless support is my safe haven.

Introduction

Hope in the Bible is something we can rely on, something that is so sure, so definite, and so solid that we can bank on it and expect it to happen without the fear of being disappointed.

Hope is a fundamental component of the life of the righteous. We can live at peace in Proverbs 23:18 'There is surely a future hope for you, and your hope will not be cut off.'

Without hope, life loses its meaning. Job certainly knew about the reality of living Hope for Today. He boldly states in Chapter 7 and verse 6 'My days are swifter than a weaver's shuttle, and they come to an end without hope.' Job suffered the great loss of his belongings, wealth, and his beloved children yet he held on to hope in God.

We find that in Romans chapter 5 verses 2 through 5, hope is produced by endurance in suffering. We can 'rejoice in the hope of the glory of God. Not only so, but we also rejoice in our sufferings, because we know that suffering produces perseverance; perseverance, character; and character, hope. And hope does not disappoint us, because God has poured out his love into our hearts by the Holy Spirit, whom he has given us.'

We can learn from First Thessalonians chapter 1 verse 3 that hope is the inspiration behind endurance 'We continually remember before our God and Father your work produced by faith, your labor prompted by love, and your endurance inspired by hope in our Lord Jesus Christ.'

Hope in Christ is the Anchor of your soul. Hebrews 6:19 in the Amplified Bible says, "[Now] we have this [hope] as a sure and steadfast anchor of the soul [it cannot slip and it cannot break down under whoever steps out upon it – a hope] that reaches farther and enters into [the very certainty of the Presence] within the veil". As an anchor holds a ship safely in position, our hope in Christ guarantees our safety and holds us securely in him. The ships anchor goes far into the depths of the water to rest on the ocean floor. Hope for the child of God goes far into the depths of the heavenly sanctuary and rests in the presence of God himself. Hope is a gift of salvation that ties us to Jesus and he goes before the Father as our representative and takes us along. Being tied to him we are given the privilege to come into the Father's presence because Christ has made provision for us through his shed blood.

God knows the plans that He has for you today. Plans to prosper you today and not to harm you today.

Plans to give you hope today and a future today! The Biblical definition of "hope" is "confident expectation". Hope is a firm assurance regarding things that are unclear and unknown. The Bible tells us in Romans 8:24-25 'For in this hope we were saved. But hope that is seen is no hope at all. Who hopes for what he already has? But if we hope for what we do not yet have, we wait for it patiently.' Hebrews 11:1 says 'Now faith is being sure of what we hope for and certain of what we do not see.'

It is my prayer that every morning you will learn to seek God's plans for your day. Begin each day with Him, reading His word, and spending time alone with God in prayer and hope will naturally bubble up inside of you. It is my prayer that the devotions in this book will encourage and inspire your daily walk with our Holy God and give you *Hope For Today*

CONTENTS

Week One

GOD IS DOING A NEW THING

Day One

"Forget the former things; do not dwell on the past. See, I am doing a new thing! Now it springs up: do you not perceive it? I am making a way in the desert and streams in the wasteland." Isaiah 43:18-19 NIV

As you journey through each day only God knows the challenges and experiences that will be yours to endure. Yesterday is gone; you cannot go back and re-live neither the good nor the bad. God wants to do something fresh and new in your life today.

His desire is to fill you daily with fresh, new hope through the presence of the Holy Spirit. He loves you so much that He will intervene in every situation throughout the coming days.

You may be dealing with tremendous hardships, pain and deep sorrow and all you can see is what is prevalent in the here and now. Don't downsize God and put him in a box as though he can only do small things for you. God is much bigger than your box and he has an awesome and significant purpose for your life! Trust God with the new thing he is doing even though you see no evidence of it.

I find great comfort when God says that he is making a way in the desert. I began to research this and found that in Isaiah 35:8 God is referring to a highway called the Way of Holiness. Isaiah prophesied in chapter 40 verse 3 that John the Baptist would come years later as a forerunner of Jesus Christ declaring that repentance, to make a radical change, is the only way to salvation and living a holy life. John's job was to prepare the way for the soon coming Christ.

I believe that God is saying that we must repent and seek forgiveness from the sins of our past and move forward. In doing this, we are preparing the way for Christ to come and perform unimaginable miracles in our lives. When all seems hopeless God will make a highway through your desert and call it the way of holiness. You have been set apart, sanctified and washed in the blood of Jesus Christ and he cannot wait to quench your thirsty soul.

Hope In Action: Never allow your yesterdays to determine your tomorrows and don't allow your inabilities to measure God's abilities in your life. Go before the Lord and repent, forget, and drink of his refreshing word as you travel down the highway he's prepared for you and thank him for the new thing he is doing in your life right now!

Day Two

"See, the former things have taken place, and new things I declare: before they spring into being I announce them to you". Isaiah 42:9 NIV

Hope In Action: Thank the Holy Father for all of the fulfilled promises in your life thus far and praise him for the new promises he plans for your life today!

Day Three

"I will open rivers in high places, and foun-
tains in the midst of the valleys: I will make
the wilderness a pool of water, and the dry
land springs of water." Isaiah 41:18 KJV

Hope In Action: Meditate today in the knowledge
that God would rather change the order of nature
than to see you lack for anything and praise him for
his never failing mercy and love!

Day Four

*"Brethren, I count not myself to have appre-
hended: but this one thing I do, forgetting
those things which are behind, and reaching
forth unto those things which are before,"
Philippians 3:13 KJV*

Hope In Action: Ask God to help you to move beyond
yesterday reaching forward to what is ahead as you
become more like Christ!

Day Five

"And I will bring the blind by a way that they knew not: I will lead them in paths that they have not known: I will make darkness light before them, and crooked things straight. These things will I do unto them, and not forsake them." Isaiah 42:16 KJV

Hope In Action: Praise God for guiding your footsteps and showing you the way when all is dark and dreary. Ask God to reveal to you any blindness of his truth so that you can be sensitive to the leadership of the Holy Spirit. Read Isaiah 26:7 and thank him that he will not forsake you!

Day Six

"Therefore if any man be in Christ, he is a new creature; old things are passed away; behold, all things are become new." 2 Corinthians 5:17 KJV

Hope In Action: Praise God that you are not the person you used to be. Continue to press into the word of God which is his mind, his personality, his character, it is the way he thinks and thank God for making you more like him everyday. Read Romans 6:1-14.

Day Seven

"And the Lord shall guide thee continually, and satisfy thy soul in drought, and make fat thy bones: and thou shalt be like a watered garden, and like a spring of water, whose waters fail not." Isaiah 58:11 KJV

Hope In Action: Rest in the security that the Lord will continually guide you and satisfy your soul in the desert places of life. God will give you the strength of a gushing water surge whose flow never runs dry!

Week Two

THE DEVIL IS A LIAR

Day One

"The thief cometh not, but for to steal, and to kill, and to destroy: I am come that they might have life, and that they might have it more abundantly." John 10:10 KJV

Our enemy is working very hard to accomplish his goals to steal, kill and destroy the work of God in the life of the believer. Satan wants to put to death every ounce of faith and hope that is within, steal the joy of our salvation and ultimately destroy our witness. But he will not win! Praise God that we are victorious through faith in Jesus Christ over the schemes of the devil. That is why the devil is so adamant about killing your faith because he does not want you to live a victorious life!

Do you struggle with attacks from the enemy to the point that you are both spiritually and physically tired from the battle? Just as you begin to claim total victory, satan claims his position in the battlefield of your mind and replays everything that is negative, destructive and hurtful.

Every time satan comes to you, remind him of the rest of today's verse! Jesus said, "I am come that they might have life, and that they might have it more abundantly!" Replace the word 'they' with your name and etch these words on your heart: Jesus said, "I am come that _____ might have life, and that _____ might have it more abundantly!"

You are a child of the most High God, you have been bought at a most precious and valuable price. I am speaking of the blood of Jesus Christ and because of this you have the power to overcome satan's attacks. Just remember there will always be combat before victory and it is faith in the risen Son of God that produces an abundant and victorious life!

Hope In Action: Ask God to help you to recognize and overcome satan's attacks today and praise him for the gift of abundant life in his son Christ Jesus! Read Romans 16:20.

Day Two

"For everyone born of God overcomes the world (sin): this is the victory that has overcome the world, even our faith" 1 John 5:4 NIV

Hope In Action: Exercise extravagant faith in God today and allow it to sanctify your heart and purify it from the world. Faith is your source of victorious power and as faith gains in strength, the world (sin) looses its power!

Day Three

...(The Devil) was a murderer from the beginning, not holding to the truth, for there is no truth in him. When he lies, he speaks his native language, for he is a liar and the father of lies. John 8:44 NIV

Jesus answered, "I am the way, the truth and the life. No one comes to the Father except through me." John 14:6 NIV

Hope In Action: Jesus is truth and our only defense against the devil. Embrace the truth by reading the word of God and meditating on it daily. The enemy's strongholds in your life are based on lies and you can combat them by saturating yourself in the truth of God's word.

Day Four

"Be self-controlled and alert. Your enemy the devil prowls around like a roaring lion looking for someone to devour." 1 Peter 5:8 NIV

Hope In Action: Be armed and ready with the sword of the Spirit, which is the Word of God because the spiritual enemy is waiting to pounce and devour. Be watchful and diligent to renounce him, this means to literally speak out against him, from accomplishing his schemes against you in the name of Jesus Christ!

Day Five

"Submit yourselves therefore to God. Resist the devil, and he will flee from you." James 4:7 KJV

Hope In Action: God wants to bless you and give you victory over the enemy but you must Submit to God and humble yourself before him. Do this with assured hope of victory and the devil will flee because he cannot withstand the stout resistance of the presence of The Lord!

Day Six

"Therefore, prepare your minds for action; be self-controlled; set your hope fully on the grace to be given you when Jesus Christ is revealed." 1 Peter 1:13 NIV

Hope in Action: Ask God to reveal to you all hindrances that would keep you from being active, diligent, determined and ready to work the Lord's business. Quiet yourself before God as you look forward with confidence in hope of absolute security in Jesus Christ! Read Romans 12:2.

Day Seven

Therefore put on the full armor God, so that when the day of evil comes, you may be able to stand your ground, and after you have done everything, to stand. Stand firm then, with the belt of truth buckled around your waist, with the breastplate of righteousness in place, and with your feet fitted with the readiness that comes from the gospel of peace. In addition to all this, take up the shield of faith, with which you can extinguish all the flaming arrows of the evil one. Take the helmet of salvation and the sword of the Spirit, which is the word of God. And pray in the Spirit on all occasions with all kinds of prayers and requests. With this in mind, be alert and always keep on praying for all the saints. Ephesians 6:13-18 NIV

The pieces of armor that Paul lists:

1. ***The Belt of Truth*** - We are to protect ourselves from satan's lies by girding ourselves with God's truth.
2. ***The Breastplate of Righteousness*** – When the devil accuses you and tries to make you feel unworthy and condemned, make sure your breastplate is in place by boldly telling him that you are now the righteousness of God. "There is therefore no condemnation to those who are in Christ Jesus". Romans 8:1 KJV

3. ***Feet Fitted with the Gospel of Peace*** – Having the proper footwear is vital in the spiritual battle. You must spiritually soak your feet in the word of God so that you will be firmly rooted and grounded in his truths. Be ready at all times to march into satan's territory with the message of God's saving grace and trample the obstacles that he has placed in your path.

4. ***The Shield of Faith*** – Faith will counteract every attack that satan brings against you and it makes ineffective his assault of firing the flaming arrows of doubt, depression, addiction, anxiety or any other attack. Victory comes by courage, and courage only comes by faith.

5. ***The Helmet of Salvation*** – Your mind should be protected at all times because this is the primary battlefield of the devil. Everything that enters your mind must be filtered through the helmet of salvation. "Let this mind be in you which was also in Christ Jesus". Philippians 2:5 KJV

6. ***The Sword of the Spirit*** – The word of God is the sword of the Spirit and Hebrews 4:12 tells us that it is sharper than any two-edged sword. You can powerfully pierce the darkness of evil when you believe God's word in your heart and speak it with your mouth. This is the weapon that Jesus used when he spoke scripture to ward off satan's attacks when tempted in the desert in Luke 4:1-13.

Paul concludes by reminding you to be a person of prayer because your intimacy with God is the very foundation of effective spiritual warfare.

Hope In Action: Commit that from this day forward you will apply this passage by putting on the whole armor of God daily so that you can boldly stand against the attacks of the devil.

Week Three

GOD IS MY PROTECTOR

Day One

He who dwelleth in the secret place of the most high shall abide (lodge) under the shadow of the Almighty. I will say of the Lord, He is my refuge and my fortress: my God; in him will I trust. Psalms 91:1-2 KJV

God cares for and loves you so much. He not only wants to spend time with you, he wants to dwell with you so intimately that you will choose him to be your protector and in him find all that you need or desire.

God promises great security through the protection of divine grace when you run to that secret place and hide away there in the shelter of his protection. Our Holy Father is looking down from His throne with arms opened wide yearning for you to run to Him. God longs for you to trust him enough that you will rest on his lap of everlasting love and settle down in his divine protection so that when you are faced with trials, danger or even death your soul will not be disappointed. When you abide in the secret place of the Most High God there is nothing in this world that can penetrate the protective shield that God has placed around your soul.

Hope In Action: Run today to your secret place in the arms of God and determine to live there in abiding trust as you rest in his shadow of mercy and grace.

Day Two

The Lord also will be a refuge for the oppressed, a refuge in times of trouble. And they who know thy name will put their trust in thee; for thou, Lord, hast not forsaken those who seek thee. Psalm 9:9-10 KJV

Hope in Action: We can pray to the Lord by calling on his name and trust his protection. The name of the Lord protects (Psalm 20:1), the name of the Lord saves (Psalm 54:1), the name of the Lord gives hope (Psalm 52:9). Rejoice in the fact that God is faithful to protect the powerless and the oppressed and he will not forsake those who look to him for protection.

Day Three

*Even to your old age and gray hairs I am He,
I am He who will sustain you. I have made
you and I will carry you; I will sustain you
and I will rescue you. Isaiah 46:4 NIV*

Hope In Action: Praise God that gray hairs or wrinkles don't diminish our value to him. We can never become too old for God to run to our rescue and carry us through the storms we are facing. From the moment of conception, God is faithful to carry and care for you until you are safe with Him in heaven some day.

Day Four

He (David) said; "The Lord is my rock, my fortress and my deliverer; my God is my rock in whom I take refuge, my shield and the horn of my salvation. He is my stronghold, my refuge and my Savior – from violent men you save me. I call to the Lord, who is worthy of praise, and I am saved from my enemies."
2 Samuel 22:2-4 NIV

Hope in Action: Praise God that he is your refuge, or hiding place, he is the shield that reflects the attacks of the enemy. Cling to your rock of hope, call out to the Lord and he will save you.

Day Five

"Because he loves me," says the Lord, "I will rescue him; I will protect him, for he acknowledges my name. He will call upon me, and I will answer him; I will be with him in trouble, I will deliver him and honor him." Psalm 91:14-15 NIV

Hope in Action: Take time today to be still and listen as God speaks this beautiful verse into your soul. Read it several times over and make it personal by inserting your name. God will protect, rescue and deliver you in times of trouble when you acknowledge who he is and love him with all your heart, mind and soul.

Day Six

And now I am no more in the world, but these are in the world, and I come to thee, Holy Father, keep through thine own name those whom thou hast given me, that they may be one, as we are. John 17:11 KJV

Hope in Action: In this passage, Jesus prays and asks the Holy Father to keep us, or protect us through his name. Spend time in prayer, thanking God that he is El Shaddai, the all-sufficient one in your life, and Jehovah Nissi, the Lord your banner. He is your source of strength and protection and all you will ever need.

Day Seven

In a desert land he found him, in a barren and howling waste. He shielded him and cared for him; he guarded him as the apple of his eye. Deuteronomy 32:10-12 NIV

…..for whoever touches you touches the apple of his eye. Zechariah 2:8 NIV

Keep me as the apple of your eye; hide me in the shadow of your wings. Psalm 17:8 NIV

Hope In Action: Re-read the above verses and make them personal by replacing each "him" and "you" with the word "me". Each scripture paints a beautiful picture of a loving God who comes to you, cares for and protects you with his shield of grace in the shadow of his wings of mercy. God cherishes you so much that he calls you the apple of his eye and because of this the enemy has to go through him before he can get to you!

Week Four

Jesus Loves Me

Day One

But God demonstrates his own love for us in this: while we were still sinners, Christ died for us. Romans 5:8 NIV

The love of Jesus Christ is unconditional, never condemning and always constant and true. It is beyond my comprehension why God would send his only son Jesus to die for a self absorbed greedy sinner like me but I am so thankful that he did!

I have found no greater comfort than when I worship God at the foot of the cross. With my eyes closed, I envision Jesus hanging on the cross. My arms are wrapped around its base as I lay in the refreshing pool of Christ's life changing blood. My heart is engulfed with his love as he speaks forgiveness and acceptance into my spirit.

Every morning I wake up drenched in the blessings of God and throughout the day he continues to shower me with renewed hope of his unconditional love. We all have days when we don't want to get out of bed and just don't want to see or talk to anyone. But even when we're grouchy, irritable and don't want to be loved, God loves us and goes so much further by proving his love all during the day.

Hope In Action: Rejoice in the fact that God loves you unconditionally and there is nothing you will ever do that can change the way he loves you. Thank our Holy Father for sending his son Jesus to die for your sins and cling to the cross as you worship him. Read Romans 8:38-39.

Day Two

The LORD delights in those who fear him, who put their hope in his unfailing love. Psalm 147:11 NIV

Hope in Action: According to The New Strong's Complete Dictionary of Bible Words, a Hebrew word for 'delight' is *mah-ad-awn, which* means delicacy or pleasure. The Greek word for 'delicacy' is *stray-nos* which means strength or to make strong. With this revelation, let us go back and translate this verse. Jehovah God receives pleasure and he makes us strong when we reverence him and we firmly wrap our cord of expectancy (hope) in his kindness, mercy and agape love!

Day Three

The Lord appeared to us in the past, saying,
"I have loved you with an everlasting love;
I have drawn you with loving-kindness".
Jeremiah 31:3 NIV

Hope in Action: Thank God for his steadfast love that continues to draw you to himself. Ask him to reveal areas of your life where you have wondered away from Him. He may have to apply pressure but throughout the process he never stops loving you and working in your best interest.

Day Four

I led them with cords of human kindness, with ties of love; I lifted the yoke from their neck and bent down to feed them. Hosea 11:4 NIV

Hope in Action: Rest in our Holy Father's arms of kindness and compassion as he tenderly lifts the yoke of oppression and defeat from your life. I know that what I am about to share is a stretch but bear with me. A musical composition is filled with notes that make chords. A tied note is one that is played only once but held throughout two or more measures, and measures compile the composition. Imagine your life as a composition in which God is playing the most beautiful harmonic music this side of heaven. His tied notes of love sound strong and loud as he holds you throughout the sweet notes as well as the sour notes!

Day Five

And so we know and rely on the love God has for us. God is love. Whoever lives in love lives in God, and God in him. In this way, love is made complete among us so that we will have confidence on the day of judgment, because in this world we are like him. There is no fear in love. But perfect love drives out fear, because fear has to do with punishment. The one who fears is not made perfect in love. 1 John 4:16-18 NIV

Hope In Action: Settle this fact in your heart: God is love and he is the one who initiates a love relationship with you and then pursues you with his love. Without this truth alive and active in your life nothing else will make sense. Make the love of God your dwelling place and you will have a transformed life that no longer recognizes the torment of fear.

Day Six

Be imitators of God, therefore, as dearly loved children and live a life of love, just as Christ loved us and gave himself up for us as a fragrant offering and sacrifice to God. Ephesians 5:1-2 NIV

Hope in Action: Jesus unselfishly imitated God's love by dying on the cross. He gave himself up for you as a fragrant offering and sacrifice to God. What aroma is your life sending up to the throne room of God? Take advantage of every opportunity you have to send sweet smelling fragrances to God by sacrificing your selfish will and ambitions. Imitate Christ by surrendering to God's will for your life and move forward in his sacrificial love.

Day Seven

So that Christ may dwell in your hearts through faith, and I pray that you, being rooted and established in love, may have power, together with all the saints, to grasp how wide and long and high and deep is the love of Christ, and to know this love that surpasses knowledge – that you may be filled to the measure of all the fullness of God.Ephesians 3:17-19 NIV

Hope in Action: Ask God to help you reach a deeper appreciation of his love for you. You know in your mind that you are loved because the Bible is filled with verses that testify to the depth of God's love but sometimes have a hard time feeling in your heart what you know in your mind. Read this passage every day and implore God to turn your head knowledge into a heart experience of his wide, long, high and deep love for you.

Week Five

God is Faithful To His Word

Day one

"He who calls you is faithful and he will do it." 1 Thessalonians 5:24 NIV

God did not send His Son to die for us and then later call us by the gospel to follow Christ, only to forget His purpose. Not at all! There may be times that you feel God leading you into a certain area only to leave you there all alone. But I am here to tell you that God has not left you!

I want to relate a personal testimony about a particular time when I felt God leading me to be the director of our local Crisis Pregnancy Center. I questioned God for a while because I had not had an abortion nor had anyone in my family. I didn't understand how I could effectively serve God and my community in this capacity. I had written and recorded a couple of pro-life songs and sang at several Georgia Right to Life events as well as our local Crisis Pregnancy Center events. I became involved in the pro-life movement through my music and God had certainly given me a heart to stand up and be a voice for the unborn child.

I surrendered to the Lord and began to serve as director and put into place certain jobs that God wanted accomplished and things were going good. I was totally centered in God's will for my life and was dancing on the mountaintop with the wind rushing through my hair. If you have ever worked or volunteered at a Crisis Pregnancy Center you know that the forces of evil are constantly wrestling with the forces of good and the spiritual battle can become very intense. As the days turned into weeks it was as if God had disappeared and left me there all alone. The winds of happiness turned into storms of doubt. I became frightened as I focused on the oceans of fear that swelled up inside of me and I was lonely and confused. It wasn't until I became tired of trying to reason with God and trust in my own strength that I cried out to him. As I sat there on that faded and worn out mountain top experience, he gently spoke into my spirit and said "Annette, I am the same God today as I was yesterday when you came to this mountain top. I will never leave you or cause harm to come to you. Your calling is still the same and I have given you wings so that you can soar, so go and do what I have called you to do!" The sweetness of God's redemption flooded my soul as I gained a fresh perspective of Hope in Christ.

Hope in Action: Know that God has not forgotten about you. Place all your trust in him thanking him for his faithfulness and your wings of faith will begin to grow as you soar into a deeper relationship with God.

Day Two

For the word of the LORD is right and true;
he is faithful in all he does. Psalm 33:4 NIV

Hope in Action: Jehovah Lord is your creator and his royal word governs all things in your life. Surrender to the Lord and place yourself under his authority because under his rule there is goodness and truth. Place your trust in God and depend on him to be faithful in every area of your life.

Day Three

*The works of his hands are faithful and just;
all his precepts are trustworthy. They are
steadfast forever and ever, done in faithfulness and uprightness. Psalm 111:7-8 NIV*

Hope in Action: The mandates or precepts of God
are found in the Holy Bible. Think of his word as a
written prescription individually given to you from
the hands of the great physician. Fill your prescription by taking your Bible, open it and ask God for
wisdom and discernment in applying his word in
your life. Confidently place your hope and trust in
the active ingredient of God's binding, immovable
and complete faithfulness.

Day Four

He is the Rock, his works are perfect, and all his ways are just. A faithful God who does no wrong, upright and just is he. Deuteronomy 32:4 NIV

Hope in Action: God is your defense and his works are carefully exact and his mode of action is always right and holy. You can be absolutely certain that our gentle God is a safe place you can run to and he will be forever faithful. Trust Him for he is perfect in all ways and give him praise for he is faithful.

Day Five

Know therefore that the Lord your God is God; he is the faithful God, keeping his covenant of love to a thousand generations of those who love him and keep his commands.
Deuteronomy 7:9 NIV

Hope in Action: Who is God to you? Is he the all-sufficient One, Master and Lord of your life? Jehovah God almighty is forever faithful in his everlasting love for you. Wisely invest time daily with God and get to know his nature and character through his names in scripture.

God knows you inside and out. If you have accepted Jesus Christ as your Savior, God knows you as his child. He knows what makes you happy, angry or sad. He knows all about your genetic makeup, your health issues and your deepest darkest secrets and dreams. God knows you by name so shouldn't you know him by his? If you are going to place your hope in God it is wise to know his personality and nature as he reveals himself to you. I have included only a few of the names of God to start you on your journey of personal study of knowing God.

Yahweh – The LORD [Exodus 3:14-15] Personal and covenant name of God, I AM THAT I AM, Redeemer.

Elohim – The supreme God, mighty in power and absolutely faithful to His word.

59

Jehovah-Jireh [Genesis 22:14] The LORD will see to it, Provider.

Jehovah-Nissi [Genesis 17:15] The LORD my Banner, Victory.

Jehovah-Shalom [Judges 6:24] The LORD is Peace.

My God My Strong Tower – [Proverbs 18:10]

My God My Restorer – [Psalm 23:3]

My God My Hope – [Psalm 71:5]

Day Six

Your kingdom is an everlasting kingdom, and your dominion endures through all generations. The Lord is faithful to all his promises and loving toward all he has made. Psalms 145:13 NIV

Hope in Action: God's royal dominion lasts forever and continues to remain constant and true. You can depend on God because his faithfulness and sovereignty exist through out all generations. Read Galatians 3:14, 2 Peter 3:9 and 2 Corinthians 1:20 and thank God for the precious promises he has so beautifully spoken in his Holy word.

Day Seven

No temptation has seized you except what is common to man. And God is faithful; he will not let you be tempted beyond what you can bear. But when you are tempted, he will also provide a way out so that you can stand up under it. 1 Corinthians 10:13 NIV

Hope in Action: Temptation itself is not sin, after all Jesus was tempted in the dessert (Matthew 4:1-11). Temptation only becomes sin when we yield to it. Temptation will come to you but God will also be there preparing the way of escape and it is your responsibility to look for and seize it. You may feel that the weight of temptation is more than you can bear and you are growing weary under the load. Memorize this verse and allow it to penetrate deep into your soul so that you will automatically trust that God is faithfully enabling you to resist and escape.

Week Six

GOD IS ALWAYS
WITH ME

Day One

Be strong and of a good courage, fear not, nor be afraid of them: for the Lord thy God, he it is that doth go with thee: he will not fail thee, nor forsake thee. Deuteronomy 31:6 KJV

These are the words that Moses spoke to the Israelites as well as his successor Joshua. They had spent 40 years in the desert with the promise of entering into the Holy Land and Joshua was destined to turn that promise into reality. Joshua was chosen by God to bring Moses' work to completion. God believed in the character and faith of these men and by trusting in the Lord and obeying him, they were victorious in sprite of great obstacles. Joshua was no stranger to miracles and he witnessed many miraculous works of God that the world would call impossible.

Hebrews 13:8 says that Jesus Christ is the same yesterday, today and forever. The same God that spoke these words to Moses and Joshua is speaking to you today and saying, "Be strong and don't be afraid because I will always go with you and I will never abandon you or leave you behind – I will always be with you." You too will be victorious no matter what comes to you in life when you trust and obey the Lord. God believes in you - you are his chosen child. Oh, if you could just believe in him as much as he believes in you!

Hope In Action: Read Deuteronomy 31:6-8 and praise our Holy Father for he is with you today just as he was with the Israelites yesterday. He will lead and guide you through to your promised land!

Day Two

But now this is what the Lord says - He who created you, O Jacob, he who formed you, O Israel: "Fear not, for I have redeemed you; I have summoned you by name, you are mine. When you pass through the waters, I will be with you; and when you pass through the rivers, they will not sweep over you. When you walk through the fire, you will not be burned; the flames will not set you ablaze.......Do not be afraid for I am with you." Isaiah 43:1-2,5a NIV

Hope In Action: Take time to meditate on the fact that God calls you by name and says, "You are mine". It is interesting to note that God said, "when you pass through or walk through" and not "if you". God knows that each of us will experience seasons when we feel we are drowning in our tears or about to be consumed by the blaze of controversy. I envision God holding each of us in his arms as he carries us through these seasons of deep waters and raging fires. We have nothing to fear because Christ is with us! Read Zephaniah 3:17.

Day Three

When my father and my mother forsake me, then the Lord [will gather me] will take me up. Psalm 27:10 KJV

Hope In Action: The Hebrew word for "gather" is *dawgar* and it means to brood over or to care for the young. David has painted a beautiful picture of the Lord's constant care. Parents are not perfect, we make mistakes and as much as we want to be with our children and protect them through every phase of life, it is just not humanly possible. But God is your constant protection and forever broods, or covers you with his mighty strong wings of grace. Read Isaiah 49:15-16 and rest in the words of hope and acceptance that God is speaking to you.

Day Four

Notwithstanding, the Lord stood with me, and strengthened me; that by me the preaching might be fully known, and that all the Gentiles might hear. And I was delivered out of the mouth of the lion. And the Lord shall deliver me from every evil work, and will preserve me unto his heavenly kingdom: to whom be glory forever and ever. Amen. 2 Timothy 4:17-18 KJV

Hope In Action: Praise God Almighty that he is by your side empowering you with boldness to speak and testify of his goodness and saving grace just as he was with Paul. A great missionary and preacher, Paul was fully aware of the Lord's presence in his life and nothing stopped him from serving the Lord. Every child of God is a minister and your life is preaching a sermon to the people you come in contact with every day. Stand up for God and be a mighty testimony for him because he is always with you and forever by your side!

Day Five

...And surely I am with you always, to the very end of the age. Matthew 28:20b NIV

Hope In Action: These words came from the lips of Jesus himself, the one who came to earth to be "God with us", to reassure you that he is always with you. When darkness presses in and you feel you are suffocating in loneliness run into the arms of Jesus and rest in his peaceful presence. Read Psalm 139:7-12.

Day Six

Today I have made you a fortified city, an iron pillar and a bronze wall to stand against the whole land against the kings of Judah, its officials, its priests and the people of the land. They will fight against you but will not overcome you, for I am with you and will rescue you, declares the Lord. Jeremiah 1:18-19 NIV

Hope In Action: A fortified (strong, hard and courageous) city is a symbol of security and an iron pillar and bronze wall signifies dignity and strength. Today God has come to your rescue and is making you strong and courageous with dignity and strength so that you can withstand the attacks of the enemy. Allow the promise of God's continuing presence to calm your fears and rejoice as you read Jeremiah 20:11.

Day Seven

So do not fear, for I am with you; do not be dismayed, for I am your God. I will strengthen you and help you; I will uphold you with my righteous right hand. Isaiah 41:10 NIV

Hope In Action: God is determined to make you strong and courageous as he steadfastly lifts you up with the holiness of his power and salvation. God loves you and is always with you and for you. Memorize 2 Timothy 1:7 and engrave it on your heart so that when you are overtaken with fear you are armed with God's word of power and love.

Week Seven

GOD IS MY REDEEMER
AND DEFENDER

Day One

Moreover, I have heard the groaning of the Israelites, whom the Egyptians are enslaving, and I have remembered my covenant. "Therefore, say to the Israelites: 'I am the LORD, and I will bring you out from under the yoke of the Egyptians. I will free you from being slaves to them, and I will redeem you with an outstretched arm and with mighty acts of judgment. I will take you as my own people, and I will be your God. Then you will know that I am the LORD your God, who brought you out from under the yoke of the Egyptians. And I will bring you to the land I swore with uplifted hand to give to Abraham, to Isaac and to Jacob. I will give it to you as a possession. I am the LORD." Exodus 6:5-8 NIV

God is described as our Redeemer 17 times in the Old Testament. The Lord's redemption not only releases you from slavery and bondage but also delivers you into freedom and joy in Christ Jesus. God hears your groans when you cry out to him in the midnight hour and will extend his strong and powerful arms of mercy and grace to comfort you.

Let's go back and take part of the above scripture and make it personal by filling in the blanks with your own struggles of bondage and burdens. "I am the LORD, and I will bring you out from under the yoke of _____. I will free you from being slaves to _____, and I will redeem you with an outstretched arm and with mighty acts of judgment. I will take you as my own people, and I will be your God. Then you will know that I am the LORD your God, who brought you out from under the yoke of _____."

According to Webster's Dictionary, the definition of "redeem" is to regain possession of by paying a price, to set free, to ransom, to rescue from sin and its penalties. The LORD, the Great I Am will free you from the shackles of un-forgiveness, unbelief, jealousy, bitterness, disobedience, and selfishness as well as addictions such as alcohol, drugs and tobacco.

Jesus says in John 8:58 that "before Abraham was, I Am", and in John 14:6, I AM THE way, THE truth, and THE life; no man cometh unto the Father, but by me." Jesus paid the ransom when he died on the cross to not only free you from eternal damnation but from bondage in which the world can entangle you. The blood of Jesus Christ is the only payment that God our Father will accept and the price has already been paid. Now God is waiting to regain possession of your whole heart, the place where he longs to dwell. The Redeemer who rescued Israel from the bonds of slavery is the same Redeemer who frees us from the bonds of sin.

Hope In Action: Read Psalm 18:16-19 and Exodus 15:13. Rest in the redeeming love and mercy that God has for you.

Day Two

*I know that my Redeemer lives, and that in
the end he will stand upon the earth. Job
19:25 NIV*

Hope In Action: Job declares that God is his Defender
and knows that ultimately God will vindicate him in
the face of all false accusations. Job knew that long
after his life had ended, God would continue to stand
and defend him. Job's hope is not in anything the
world or friends provide but only in God. Continue
to be sensitive to the still, small voice of God and
trust that his ways are right and perfect. Just as Job
didn't understand all that was going on in his life, you
won't either but just as Job declared and believed,
my Redeemer (defender) lives and will vindicate me,
you must also!

Day three

Their Redeemer is strong; the LORD of hosts is his name; he shall thoroughly plead their cause, that he may give rest to the land, and disquiet the inhabitants of Babylon. Jeremiah 50:34 KJV

Hope In Action: The LORD is Great and Mighty and the only one with strength and endurance enough to hold you in his redeeming arms as he pleads your case and in doing this he gives you rest. Did you get that? He gives rest to his redeemed and unrest to the wicked. Are you having periods of unrest in certain areas of your life? Ask God to search your heart and reveal the areas that need redemption. Repent and pray for God's forgiveness and allow him to regain possession and he will give you rest even in the most difficult circumstances you may face.

Day Four

*Let the redeemed of the LORD say so, whom
he hath redeemed from the hand of the enemy.
Psalm 107:2 KJV*

Hope In Action: Take time to go back over your life
and recall occasions where God delivered you from
things that could have corrupted or ruined your life.
Think of the strongholds he tore down and the times
he has picked you up and snatched you from the
clutches of the enemy. Praise the Lord that through
his unfailing love he hears your prayers of need and
runs to redeem you.

Day Five

My lips will shout for joy when I sing praise to you – I, whom you have redeemed. Psalm 71:23 NIV

Hope In Action: Read the entire chapter of Psalm 71 and allow the words of David to encourage you as he appeals for help, confesses hope in the Sovereign Lord and vows to praise him in anticipation of deliverance. David teaches us that praise must be conceived in redemption just as prayer is conceived in the time of need.

Day Six

The LORD redeems his servants; no one will be condemned who takes refuge in him. Psalm 34:22 NIV

Hope In Action: Be assured that God hears the prayers of the righteous and he is your unfailing deliverer. Take refuge in God's redeeming love and praise him that you were not dealt with as guilty. Read verses 17-19 of chapter 34. God is pleased when we humbly approach him with a heart that pleads for mercy especially when sin has been committed.

Day Seven

For you know that it was not with perishable things such as silver or gold that you were redeemed from the empty way of life handed down to you from your forefathers, but with the precious blood of Christ, a lamb without blemish or defect. 1 Peter 1:18-19 NIV

Hope In Action: Think about what the phrase "empty way of life" means to you. You may be unhappy and feel that your life is not satisfying enough. Maybe you have a history of destructive behavior in your family and you have found yourself going down that same road. Stop right now, turn around and run to Jesus! Oh, if you could comprehend how valuable you are to him. God owns every ounce of gold and silver in this world and he would have gladly taken all of it for your ransom but so much more was required - the blood of his perfect son, Jesus Christ. Look with your heart at his hands and feet that are nailed to the cross, blood streaming to the ground and his body convulsing with pain. Read Titus 2:12-14 and walk in the freedom that only redemption from God can give.

Week Eight

I AM FORGIVEN

Day One

Blessed is he whose transgressions are forgiven, whose sins are covered. Blessed is the man whose sin the LORD does not count against him and in whose spirit is no deceit. When I kept silent, my bones wasted away through my groaning all day long. For day and night your hand was heavy upon me; my strength was sapped as in the heat of summer. Then I acknowledged my sin to you and did not cover up my iniquity. I said, "I will confess my transgressions to the LORD" – and you forgave the guilt of my sin! Psalm 32:1-5 NIV

God's beautiful gift of forgiveness is yours to keep when you surrender to him confess your sins and are receptive to his authority in your life. You must be honest with God in order to receive the fullness of this gift. The stubborn silence of unacknowledged sin leads to a life filled with groaning and complaining. You will be utterly exhausted and spiritually, emotionally and even physically drained.

The Psalmist David was considered a man after God's own heart (1 Samuel 13:14) and yet he struggled with sin but he knew the freedom that was wrapped in God's gift of forgiveness. David teaches us that God is always ready to forgive and sweet relief comes with a full and honest confession.

Hope In Action: Read proverbs 28:13 and bask in the joy that follows God's forgiveness. Acknowledge your sins before the Lord and separate, or disown, yourself from them and then Praise God for showering you with his bountiful mercy!

Day Two

*If we confess our sins, he is faithful and just
to forgive us our sins, and to cleanse us from
all unrighteousness. 1 John 1:9 KJV*

Hope In Action: God's response toward those who
confess their sins is in accordance to his tender
nature of faithfulness and righteousness. According
to The New Strong's Complete Dictionary of Bible
Words, one of the Greek definitions for the word
'forgive' is *apŏluō* and it means to free fully, let die,
pardon, send away, release and set at liberty. Read
1 Peter 2:24 and Romans 6:3-14. Ask God to give
you a fresh understanding of forgiveness concerning
Christ's death and resurrection and your death to sin.
Be still and rest in God's promise of forgiveness that
restores your relationship with The Holy Father.

Day Three

*As far as the east is from the west, so far
has he removed our transgressions from us.
Psalm 103:12 NIV*

Hope In Action: God not only puts our sins out of
sight but he also puts them out of reach, out of mind,
and out of total existence. David used the analogy of
the world's boundaries to help us grasp the vast great-
ness of our Lord's forgiving grace. Read Isaiah 38:17
and meditate on the fact that when God forgives you
from sin, he places it behind him and never looks
back.

Day Four

Who is a God like you, who pardons sin and forgives the transgression of the remnant of his inheritance? You do not stay angry forever but delight to show mercy. You will again have compassion on us; you will tread out sins underfoot and hurl all out iniquities into the depths of the sea. Micah 7:18-19 NIV

Hope In Action: The name *Micah* means "Who is like the LORD?" Micah begins this scripture by asking the Lord – Who is a God like you who is majestic in holiness, awesome in glory, forgives our sin and releases us from deserved punishment. God's nature is to restore and it is his pleasure to reveal his kindness, favor and compassion to you. Rejoice in the God who shows mercy without anger, forgives with compassion, and remembers our transgressions no more as if he hurled them into the deepest part of the sea.

Day Five

The Holy Spirit also testifies to us about this. First he says: "This is the covenant I will make with them after that time, says the Lord. I will put my law in their hearts, and I will write them on their minds." Then he adds: "Their sins and lawless acts I will remember no more." And where these have been forgiven, there is no longer any sacrifice for sin. Hebrews 10:15-18 NIV

Hope In Action: Rest in the Holy Spirit's testimony that your sins will be completely forgiven and that no additional sacrifice is needed. Jesus, the spotless Lamb of God, was the only sacrifice that was acceptable and needful. God's law is found in his word, the Holy Bible and it becomes imbedded in your heart and mind when you memorize it. Praise God that when he forgives it becomes an everlasting reality!

Day Six

If you, O LORD, kept a record of sins, O Lord, who could stand? But with you there is forgiveness; therefore you are feared. Psalm 130:3-4 NIV

Hope In Action: Even when we deliberately sin God hears our cries for help, takes us in and forgives! Our Holy Father is compassionate and gracious in mercy. Praise God that although he keeps a record of every tear we cry (Psalm 56:8) he does just the opposite with confessed and forgiven sins! Confidently trust in the Lord as you read all eight verses of Psalm 130.

Day Seven

For he has rescued us from the dominion of darkness and brought us into the kingdom of the Son he loves, in whom we have redemption, the forgiveness of sins. Colossians 1:13-14 NIV

Hope In Action: The child of God is no longer under the dominion of evil or darkness but under the perfect rule of Jesus Christ, the son whom God loves. Praise God for rescuing you when he sent his son Jesus to pay your ransom and rejoice in God's forgiveness, deliverance and freedom.

Week Nine

GOD IS ALL POWERFUL

Day One

Ascribe to the LORD, O mighty ones, ascribe to the LORD glory and strength. Ascribe to the LORD the glory due his name; worship the LORD in the splendor of his holiness. The voice of the LORD is over the waters; the God of glory thunders, the LORD thunders over the mighty waters. The voice of the LORD is powerful; the voice of the Lord is majestic. The voice of the LORD breaks the cedars; the Lord breaks in pieces the cedars of Lebanon. He makes Lebanon skip like a calf, Sirion like a young wild ox. The voice of the LORD strikes with flashes of lightening. The voice of the LORD shakes the desert; The LORD shakes the Desert of Kadesh. The voice of the LORD twists the oaks and strips the forests bare. And in his temple all cry, "Glory!" The LORD sits enthroned over the flood; the LORD is enthroned as King forever. The LORD gives strength to his people; the LORD blesses his people with peace. Psalm 29 NIV

The Pvsalmist David wrote this beautiful hymn of praise to the Lord whose power and majesty are not only visible through creation but also audible in creations most awesome voice through thunderbolts and lightening flashes. The voice of God rides on the clouds proclaiming His glory! God speaks and the raging waters obey as He sits enthroned over the earth showering his people with strength and peace. God speaks with power and authority and his voice alone is like a refreshing pool of water in the dry desert.

"The voice of the LORD" is repeated seven times in this chapter and seven is the number of completion. Claim the power of God in every area of your life and when he speaks cherish it as the absolute truth that will come to completion in his time.

Hope In Action: The Lord's committed perfect and absolute authority over his people covers us with a cloak of comfort in a world where threatening storms and chaos make everything uncertain. Acknowledge that the Lord alone is the divine King and he alone is worthy of your worship. Read Isaiah 45:5-7.

Day Two

Yet he (Abraham) did not waver through unbelief regarding the promise of God, but was strengthened in his faith and gave glory to God, being fully persuaded that God had power to do what he had promised. Romans 4:20-21 NIV

Hope In Action: Through the strength of Abraham's faith he gave glory to God because he believed that God would do what he promised. Abraham had complete confidence in the power of God to fulfill his promise of a child. Trust and believe that the same God who birthed a nation through a couple that was 90 and 100 years old is just as powerful today to birth his promises in your life. All circumstances surrounding you say it is impossible but with God all things are possible! Read Matthew 19:26.

Day Three

Ah Lord God! Behold, thou hast made the heaven and the earth by thy great power and stretched out arm, and there is nothing too hard for thee. Jeremiah 32:17 KJV

Hope In Action: Praise God that nothing including creation and redemption is too hard for him! God is supremely powerful and trust him to always be your defender and rest in his powerful arms that reaches all the way to you.

Day Four

His divine power has given us everything we need for life and godliness through our knowledge of him who called us by his own glory and goodness. 2 Peter 1:3 NIV

Hope In Action: There is no secret or hidden formula to the knowledge of God. Notice this verse says, "His divine power has given" which means that we already hold in our possession everything we need! According to The new Strong's Complete Dictionary of Bible Words, the Greek transliteration for *knowledge is "epiginosko"* which means to become fully acquainted with. As we become fully acquainted through prayer and Bible study with the one who called us by his glory and goodness, which are his attributes of excellence, his divine power has given us everything we need for life and godliness!

Day Five

For the word of God is quick [living], and powerful, and sharper than any twoedged sword, piercing even to the dividing asunder of soul and spirit, and of the joints and marrow, and is a discerner [able to judge] of the thoughts and intents [intentions] of the heart. Hebrews 4:12 KJV

Hope In Action: Amen! The word of God is truth and was revealed through Jesus Christ (John 1:1,14). The word of God is made alive today through the Holy Bible and the Holy Spirit living inside each one of us. The living word of God powerfully judges his children with an all-seeing eye that penetrates deep into the soul and spirit of each one of us. Pray the above verse asking God to perform spiritual surgery to remove everything that is unrighteous and unholy. Read and pray Psalm 51.

Day Six

But he said to me, "My grace is sufficient for you, for my power is made perfect in weakness." Therefore I will boast all the more gladly about my weaknesses, so that Christ's power may rest on me. 2 Corinthians 12:9 NIV

Hope In Action: Human weakness provides the opportunity for God to display his divine power. Memorize the above verse along with Philippians 4:13.

Day Seven

You are the God who performs miracles;
you display your power among the peoples.
Psalm 77:14 NIV

Hope In Action: Take a moment and reflect on the miracles that God has performed in your life and in the lives of family members and friends. Only our precious all-powerful God can heal a body of terminal sickness, break the bondage of addition or supply the amount of money needed to pay a bill or buy groceries. And God alone, the One and Only all-powerful Savior accomplishes the miracle of salvation when he comes to dwell in your heart and make it his home.

Week Ten

MY LIFE HAS PURPOSE
AND MEANING

Day One

For I know the thoughts that I think toward you, saith the LORD, thoughts of peace, and not of evil [calamity], to give you an expected end [a future and a hope]. Jeremiah 29:11 KJV

We find in this verse the message of hope, comfort and confidence that God has a definite plan and purpose for each one of us. God knows the future and what is best for us and therefore desires that we trust him.

God foreknows the design that he intentionally anticipates for your life and the foundation of this design is built on hope, peace, and prosperity in time to come. Although misfortune and disaster may come your way, they are not ultimately God's desire for your life.

Jeremiah sends a letter from Jerusalem to the Babylonian exiles that tells the captives to settle down, build houses, plant gardens, pray for the land and to move ahead with their lives. The Lord promised that after they had lived in exile seventy years he would return his people to their homeland. God declared with sweet assurance that he had not forgotten about his people.

Maybe you can relate to the abandoned captive or you're growing tired of waiting for dreams that seem to be fading into your hopes of yesterday. God has not forgotten about you - don't give up! Although your situation seems grim, keep praying and seek the Lord with your whole heart because your life has purpose and meaning! God promises his ever abiding presence, protection, strength and hope for your future!

Hope In Action: Read Jeremiah 29:11-14. Spend time alone with God in thanksgiving and praise. Although your circumstances are yelling misfortune and ruin, run into the arms of Jesus and rest in his promised peace. You will find that prosperity is within you when you seek the Lord and delight in his presence.

Day Two

*And we know that all things work together for
good to them that love God, to them who are
the called according to his purpose. Romans
8:28 KJV*

Hope In Action: We can be absolutely assured that
God works together all circumstances for good in the
life of the believer. This does not say that everything
works for our pleasure and enjoyment. The Greek
transliteration for the word "good" is kals and it means
beautiful or valuable and is used seventy eight times
in scripture. God makes everything work together
in your life to make you more beautiful and more
valuable to him. Jesus exemplifies a life of beauty
and value and you can rest assured that everything
that happens in your life from complete happiness
to heart-wrenching sorrow has one purpose and that
is to make you more like him. God does not change
his mind in reference to his call, you are his and he is
constantly working to make you more like him.

Day Three

For you created my inmost being; you knit me together in my mother's womb. I praise you because I am fearfully and wonderfully made; you works are wonderful, I know that full well. My frame was not hidden from you when I was made in the secret place. When I was woven together in the depths of the earth, your eyes saw my unformed body. All the days ordained for me where written in your book before one of them came to be. Psalm 139:13-16 NIV

Hope In Action: There is absolutely nothing about you that God doesn't know so there is nothing that you can do or even think about that will surprise him or cause him to abandon you. You are not here by accident. Our wise and sovereign God carefully planned your life with purpose and meaning. Read Psalm 119:73-74.

Day Four

And provide for those who grieve in Zion – to bestow on them a crown of beauty instead of ashes, the oil of gladness instead of mourning, and a garment of praise instead of a spirit of despair. They will be called oaks of righteousness, a planting of the LORD for the display of his splendor. I delight greatly in the LORD; my soul rejoices in my God, for he has clothed me with garments of salvation and arrayed me in a robe of righteousness. Isaiah 61:3,10 NIV

Hope In Action: God runs to your rescue and take a cloth of grace drenched in his anointing and washes away the ruins of mourning and despair that has consumed you. He sets you up and shows you off as evidence of his redemptive work! Read Psalm 30:5 and praise God that weeping may last through the night but joy comes in the morning.

Day Five

But now, O LORD, thou art our father; we are the clay, and thou our potter; and we all are the work of thy hand. Isaiah 64:8 KJV

Hope In Action: Take time to meditate on this verse and consider the fact that you are of the utmost importance to God. You are a miracle wonderfully formed and created by your loving Holy Father and he does not waste time on things that are of no importance or significance.

Day Six

But you are a chosen people, a royal priest-hood, a holy nation, a people belonging to God, that you may declare the praises of him who called you out of darkness into his wonderful light. 1 Peter 2:9 NIV

Hope In Action: As a child of God you belong to him. You have been set apart and chosen to be a royal priesthood and you are a recipient of God's mercy and grace. Read Psalm 43:3-5 and rest in the hope of God as you praise him for rescuing you from darkness. Allow the light of his word to guide you in his ways.

Day Seven

Remain in me, and I will remain in you. No branch can bear fruit by itself; it must remain in the vine. Neither can you bear fruit unless you remain in me. I am the vine; you are the branches. If a man remains in me and I in him, he will bear much fruit; apart from me you can do nothing. You did not choose me, but I chose you and appointed you to go and bear fruit – fruit that will last. Then the Father will give you whatever you ask in my name. John 15:4-5,16 NIV

Set your minds on things above, not on earthly things. And whatever you do, whether in word or deed, do it all in the name of the Lord Jesus, giving thanks to God the Father through him. Colossians 3:2,17 NIV

Hope In Action: The Hebrew word for both "remain" and "set" is *shaw-kan* and means to reside or permanently stay, have habitation or to rest in. The primary purpose for the child of God is to permanently stay in Christ therefore visibly bearing his characteristics. In doing this, others will see that your accomplishments are made only possible through Christ that lives in you. A branch out of contact with the vine is lifeless and a living union with Christ, the vine, is absolutely

necessary for without it life has no meaning. Read
Galatians 5:22.

May the God of hope fill you with all joy and peace as you trust in him, so that you may overflow with hope by the power of the Holy Spirit. Romans 15:13 NIV

Printed in the United States
203668BV00001B/1-258/P

9 781606 474334